U.S.A. TRAVEL GUIDES

MASSACHUSETTS

BY ANN HEINRICHS • ILLUSTRATED BY MATT KANIA

The Child's World®
childsworld.com

Published by The Child's World®
1980 Lookout Drive • Mankato, MN 56003-1705
800-599-READ • www.childsworld.com

Photo Credits
Photographs ©: Christian Delbert/Shutterstock Images, cover, 1; Denis Tangney Jr./iStockphoto, 7, 32; Jia Wang Kun/Shutterstock Images, 8; Gene Krebs/iStockphoto, 11; Everett Historical/Shutterstock Images, 12; Robert Linsdell CC2.0, 15; Sean Pavone/Shutterstock Images, 16; Charles Goodman/Library of Congress, 17; Pendleton's Lithography/Library of Congress, 18 (top left); Library of Congress, 18 (top right); Cecil Stoughton/White House, 18 (bottom left); IIP Photo Archive CC2.0, 18 (bottom right); Jeffrey M. Frank/Shutterstock Images, 19; Richard Howe CC2.0, 20; Joseph Sohm/Shutterstock Images, 23; z0rc CC2.0, 24; Travis Blue/iStockphoto, 27; Kenneth Wiedemann/iStockphoto, 28; Al Ravenna/New York World-Telegram and the Sun Newspaper Photograph Collection /Library of Congress, 30; MBR/KRT/Newscom, 31; Shutterstock Images, 35, 37 (top), 37 (bottom)

ISBN 9781503819610
LCCN 2016961174

Printing
Printed in the United States of America
PA02334

post card

About the Author
Ann Heinrichs

Ann Heinrichs is the author of more than 100 books for children and young adults. She has also enjoyed successful careers as a children's book editor and an advertising copywriter. Ann grew up in Fort Smith, Arkansas, and lives in Chicago, Illinois.

post card

About the
Map Illustrator
Matt Kania

Matt Kania loves maps and, as a kid, dreamed of making them. In school he studied geography and cartography, and today he makes maps for a living. Matt's favorite thing about drawing maps is learning about the places they represent. Many of the maps he has created can be found in books, magazines, videos, Web sites, and public places.

On the cover: The Massachusetts coast is lined with historic lighthouses.

OUR MASSACHUSETTS TRIP

MASSACHUSETTS

Y ou're in for a great tour of the Bay State! Just follow the dotted line—or else skip around. Either way, you'll have lots of fun. You'll learn some amazing things, too. You'll meet Samuel Adams and Dr. Seuss. You'll see whales and witches and parades. You'll follow Paul Revere on his midnight ride. Are you ready? Then buckle up, and let's hit the road!

WELCOME TO
MASSACHUSETTS

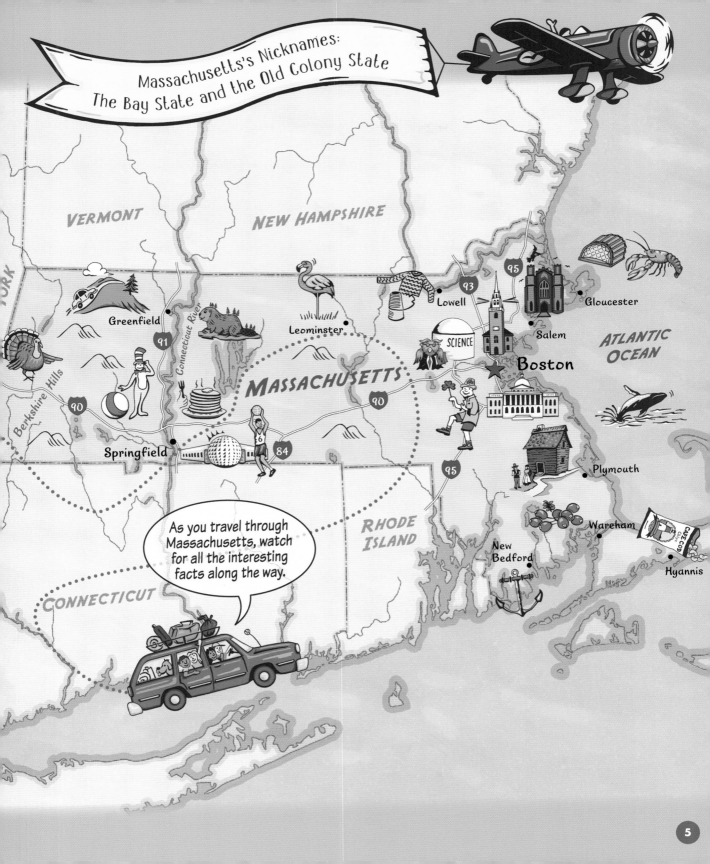

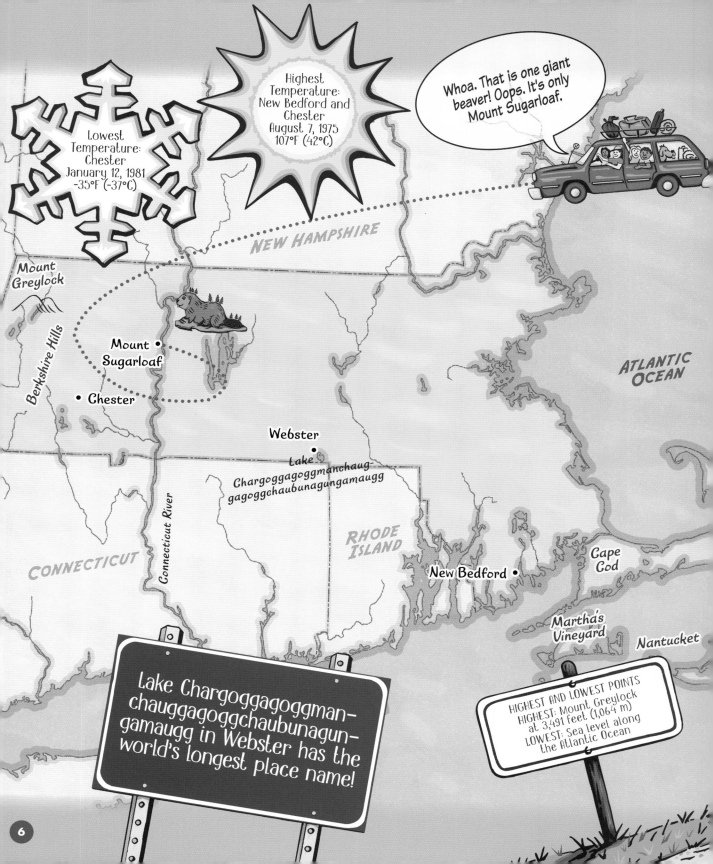

MOUNT SUGARLOAF AND THE HILLS AND COAST

Native American legends say Mount Sugarloaf is a giant beaver's body. Mount Sugarloaf is by the Connecticut River. The river runs down Massachusetts from north to south. It cuts a fertile valley through the state. The Berkshire Hills are in western Massachusetts. Lots of snow covers the slopes in the winter.

Eastern Massachusetts faces the Atlantic Ocean. The coast is partly sandy and partly rocky. The southeast coast curls up like a fishhook. It's called Cape Cod. Lots of islands lie offshore. The biggest islands are Martha's Vineyard and Nantucket.

Mount Sugarloaf is a great place to see the colors of fall.

WHALE WATCHING IN PROVINCETOWN

Want a close-up look at some whales? Just take a whale-watching boat trip. Boats leave from Provincetown, Gloucester, and other coastal towns.

Whales, dolphins, and lots of fish swim off the coast. Lobsters and crabs live out there, too. You'll see pelicans and gulls along the shore.

Forests cover more than half the state. Deer, foxes, and wild turkeys live there. Remember the giant beaver? Those beavers really lived in Massachusetts long ago. They were as big as bears! Today, a beaver could fit in your backpack. Now, don't get any bright ideas!

Keep your eyes peeled! You wouldn't want to miss seeing a whale.

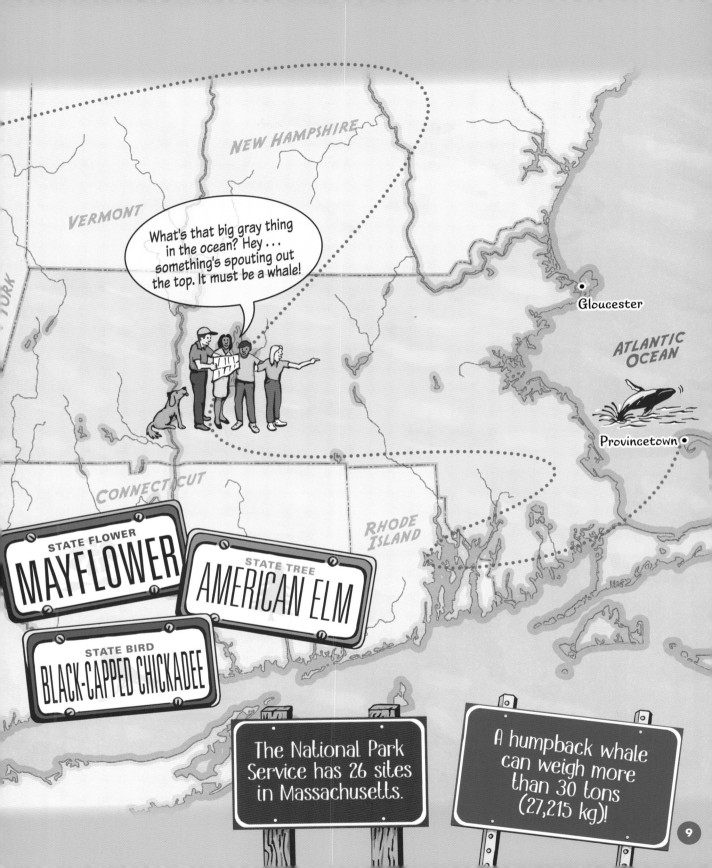

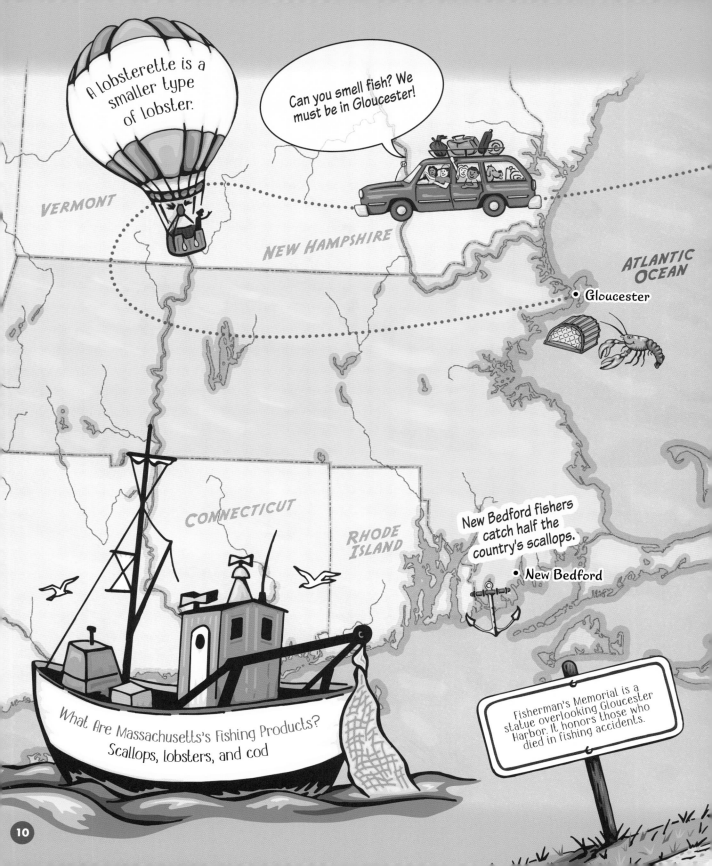

FISHING BOATS IN GLOUCESTER

Fishing boats are lined up in Gloucester Harbor. They catch fish and lobsters. It's fun to watch the lobster fishers. They sink wooden lobster traps into the sea. Then they come back later to collect their lobsters. How can they find their traps? They tie balloons or plastic jugs on them. These float on top of the water.

Fishing is a big business in Massachusetts. Gloucester and New Bedford are the best fishing ports. Fishers haul in cod, flounder, tuna, and other fish. Some catch shellfish such as scallops, clams, and crabs. Squid is another catch. Do you like squid? Try frying it. It tastes great!

Gloucester Harbor is part of Massachusetts's North Shore.

PLYMOUTH AND THE PLIMOTH PLANTATION

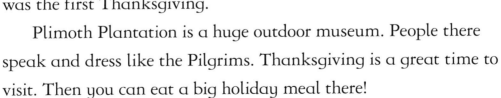

Plymouth was the first permanent English **settlement** in Massachusetts. (It was spelled "Plimoth" at the time.) The Pilgrims started it in 1620. They hunted and grew crops. The Wampanoag helped them. They all shared a big meal after the harvest. That was the first Thanksgiving.

Plimoth Plantation is a huge outdoor museum. People there speak and dress like the Pilgrims. Thanksgiving is a great time to visit. Then you can eat a big holiday meal there!

The first Thanksgiving was almost 400 years ago!

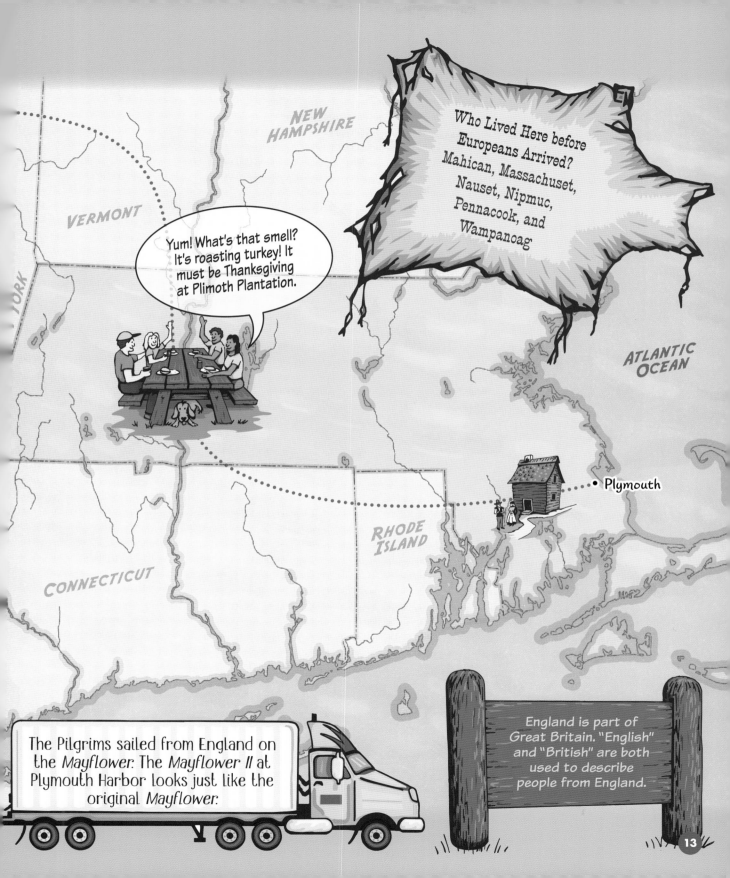

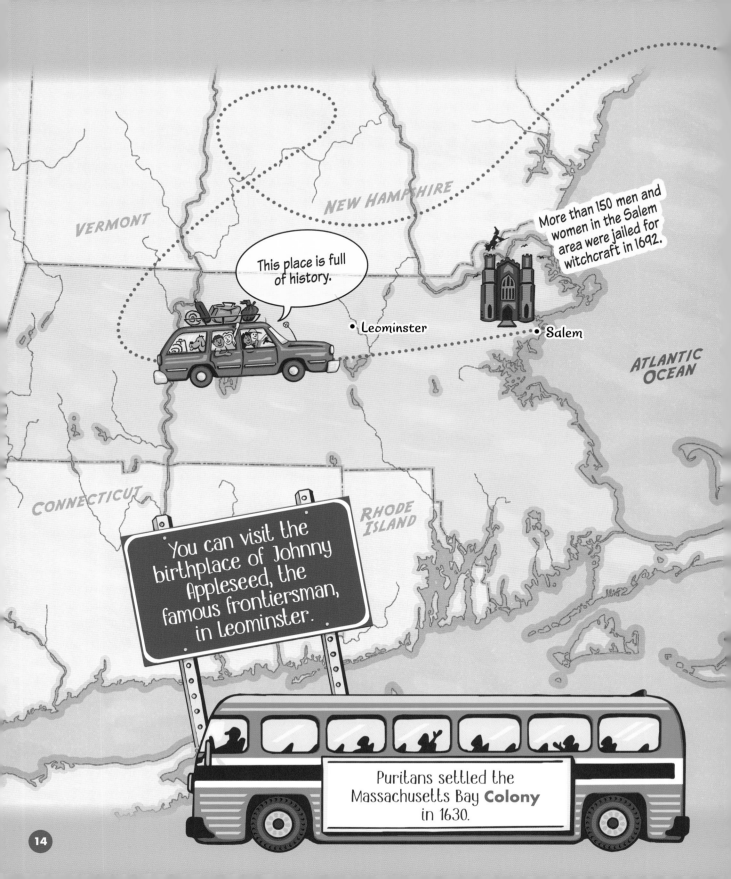

THE SALEM WITCH MUSEUM

Part of Massachusetts's early history isn't so nice. Throughout the 1600s, people continued to settle in Massachusetts. Many of these people were Puritans. They were a strict religious group.

The town of Salem was founded in 1626. In the late 1690s, some young girls became unexplainably sick. The Puritans grew very suspicious and paranoid. Wanting an answer to their problems, they turned to blame. The only logical answer for them at the time? Witchcraft.

Dozens of people were accused of being witches. They went to trial. The trials were not fair. Nineteen people were sentenced to death and hanged.

Now a museum in Salem is dedicated to the Salem Witch Trials. Stop by to learn about all of this history and more.

The Salem Witch Museum shows visitors what happened in 1692.

PAUL REVERE AND THE OLD NORTH CHURCH

As legend goes, it was almost midnight on April 18, 1775. Paul Revere knew that British soldiers were coming to Boston. The colonies wanted freedom from British rule. Now Britain was sending soldiers. But were they coming over land or in boats? Revere watched the **steeple** of Boston's Old North Church. A **lookout** would hang lanterns there—"One if by land, two if by sea."

At last, Revere saw the signal that the British were coming by sea. He had to warn people. He sprang onto his horse and dashed off into the night.

British soldiers came the very next day. They exchanged gunfire with the **colonists** in Lexington and Concord. That began the Revolutionary War (1775–1783). The colonies won. They became the United States of America.

A statue of Paul Revere now stands in Boston. Look closely—you can see the Old North Church in the back!

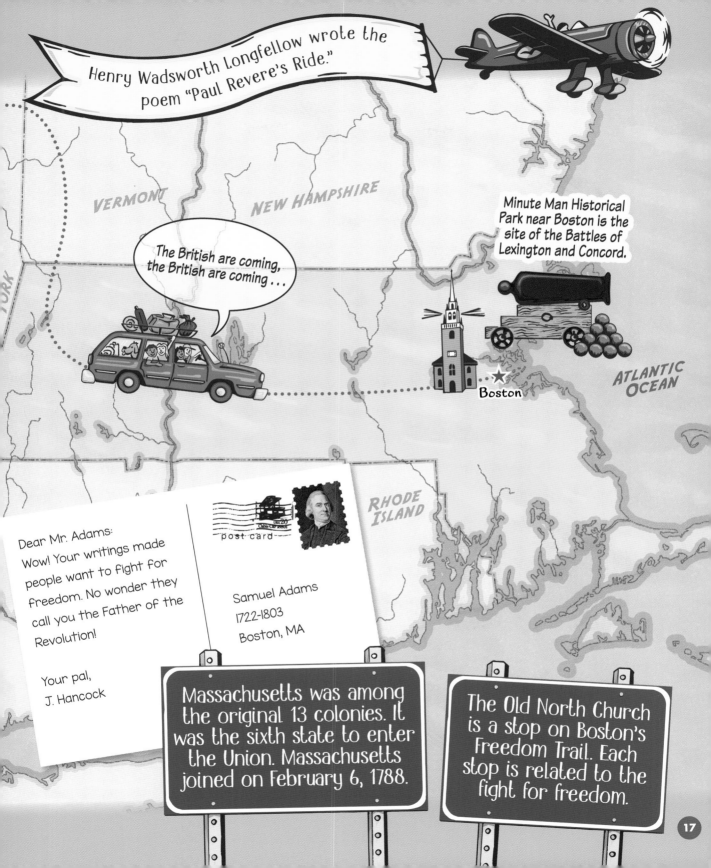

Henry Wadsworth Longfellow wrote the poem "Paul Revere's Ride."

VERMONT

NEW HAMPSHIRE

The British are coming, the British are coming . . .

Minute Man Historical Park near Boston is the site of the Battles of Lexington and Concord.

Boston

ATLANTIC OCEAN

RHODE ISLAND

YORK

post card

Dear Mr. Adams:
Wow! Your writings made people want to fight for freedom. No wonder they call you the Father of the Revolution!

Your pal,
J. Hancock

Samuel Adams
1722-1803
Boston, MA

Massachusetts was among the original 13 colonies. It was the sixth state to enter the Union. Massachusetts joined on February 6, 1788.

The Old North Church is a stop on Boston's Freedom Trail. Each stop is related to the fight for freedom.

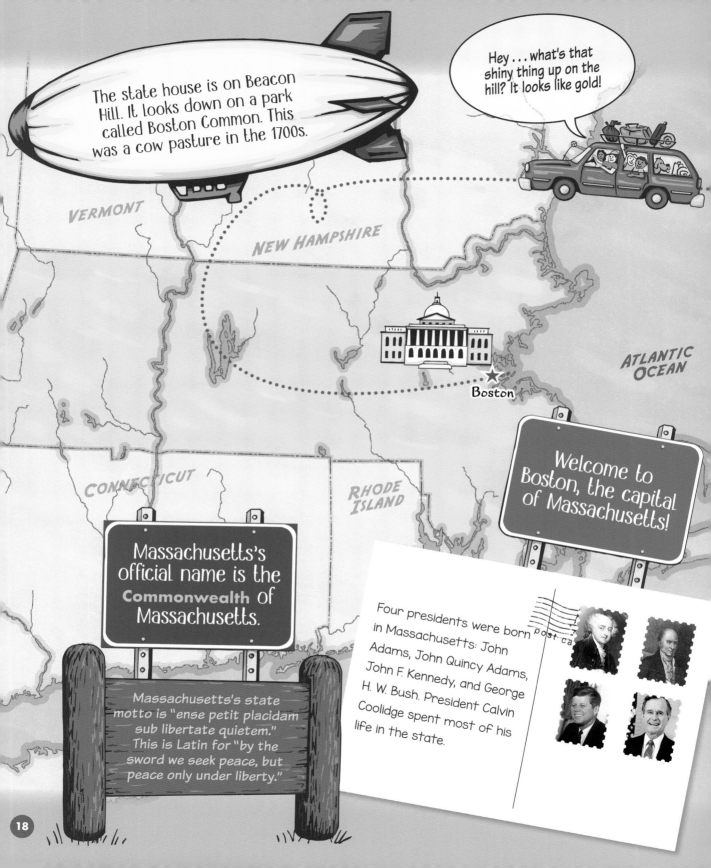

THE STATE HOUSE IN BOSTON

The Massachusetts State House has a golden dome. You can see it glistening for miles. It's coated with a thin layer of real gold!

Inside the state house are government offices. The state government has three branches. One branch makes laws. The governor heads another branch. It carries out the laws. Courts make up the third branch. They decide if laws have been broken.

The Massachusetts State House is the oldest building on Beacon Hill. Talk about history!

BOOTT COTTON MILLS MUSEUM IN LOWELL

Mills were the first factories in Massachusetts. They made cloth, shoes, and boots. Each mill stood beside a river. The flowing water turned a giant wheel. That made the mill's machine parts run.

Lots of **immigrants** worked at the mills. So did women and young girls. They worked long hours. The mills were noisy and dusty. Mill workers got very tired.

Check out Boott Cotton Mills Museum in Lowell. You'll learn about the people who worked there. You can try spinning and weaving cotton, too. Just put on your apron and get to work!

Boott Cotton Mills closed its doors as a factory in 1955.

What a racket! Is that thunder? No, it's the weaving machines at Boott Cotton Mills.

VERMONT

NEW HAMPSHIRE

YORK

• Lowell

• Sterling

ATLANTIC OCEAN

CONNECTICUT

RHODE ISLAND

Lowell was known for its **textile** mills. It was the birthplace of America's Industrial Revolution. That's when people began making things in factories.

The poem "Mary Had a Little Lamb" was about Mary Sawyer of Sterling. Her pet lamb really did follow her around.

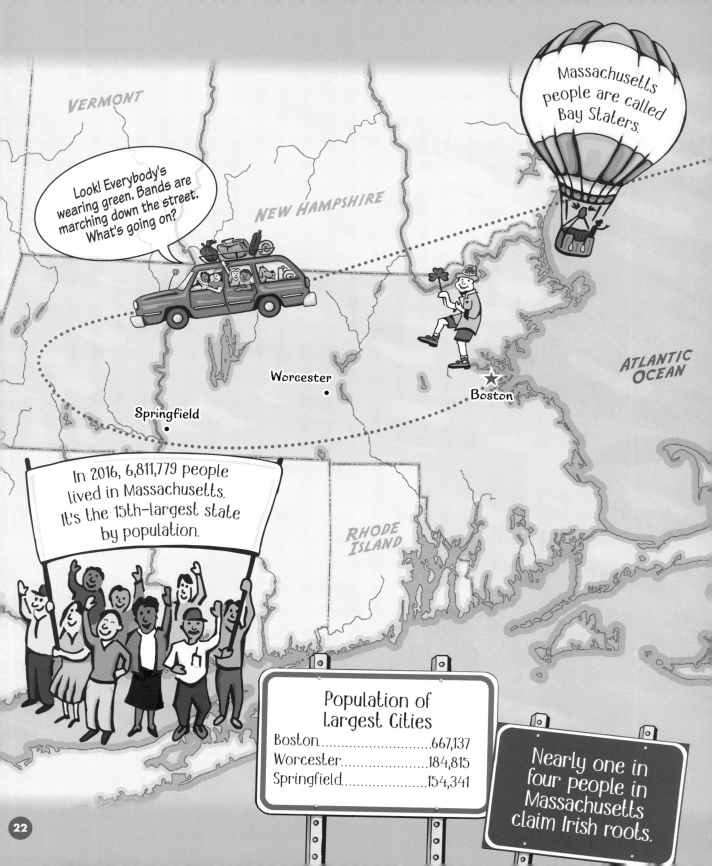

THE SAINT PATRICK'S DAY PARADE

It's the Saint Patrick's Day parade! Boston has a big parade for Saint Patrick's Day, March 17. That's because so many Bay Staters have Irish roots. Saint Patrick is the patron saint of Ireland.

Why wear green on Saint Patrick's Day? Because the shamrock, or three-leaf clover, is green. That's Ireland's unofficial national plant.

Lots of other Bay Staters are Italian or French-Canadian. Their grandparents might have worked in the mills. But that's just part of the picture. Bay Staters are like a big patchwork quilt. Their **ancestors** came from many different countries!

Lots of people enjoy dressing up for the Saint Patrick's Day parade in Boston.

BOSTON'S MUSEUM OF SCIENCE

The Human Hall of Life is a great place to visit. It's an exhibit at the Boston's Museum of Science. You'll learn all about the biology of the human body. Check out some of the museum's other exhibits, too. You can build, invent, and create things. Do you like math and science games? There are plenty of those, too.

Computers and science are important in Massachusetts. The mills were slowing down by the 1950s. Luckily, Massachusetts had many people who worked in science and technology. Some designed rockets and spacecraft. Others worked on computers. They opened up many new **industries**. Many attended the Massachusetts Institute of Technology (MIT). It opened way back in 1861. A lot of discoveries have been made there.

The museum has many exhibits—including some on dinosaurs!

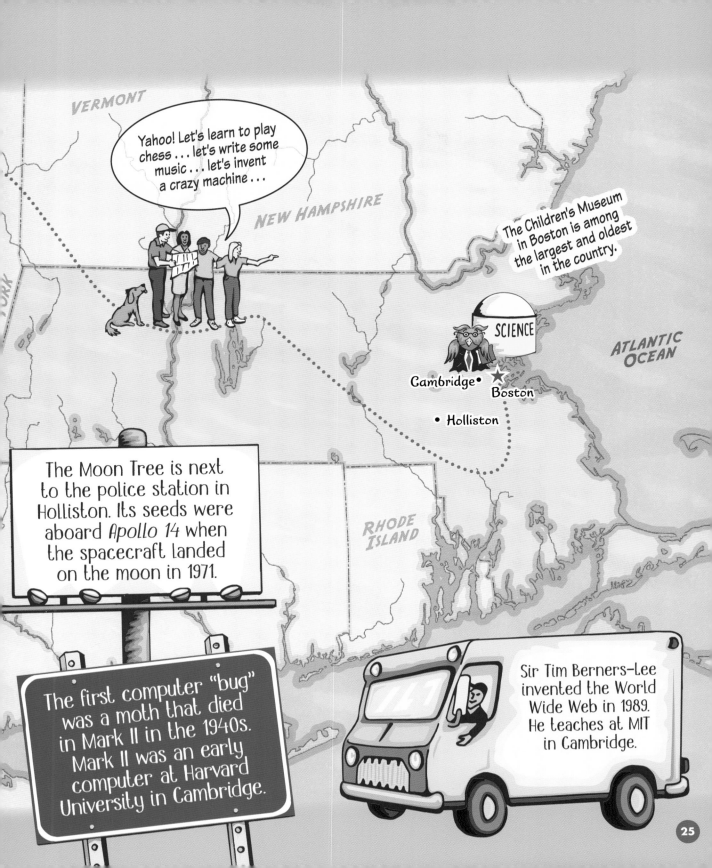

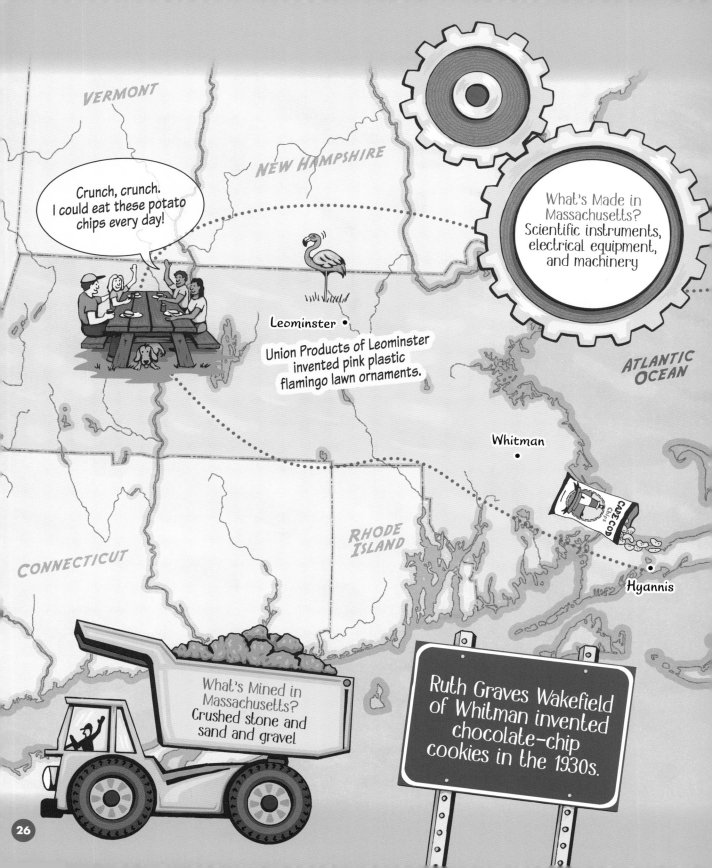

CAPE COD POTATO CHIPS IN HYANNIS

ape Cod Potato Chips are made in Hyannis. You can tour the potato chip factory. It makes 150,000 bags of crunchy snacks every day! You'll see machines peel and slice potatoes. Then the slices are fried till they're nice and crispy. And you get free potato chips, too. Just don't talk with your mouth full!

At first, Massachusetts's factories made cloth and shoes. Now the state's factories make lots of things. You can't eat them all. But you probably use them. They include tools, computers, and medicines.

There's nothing better than eating a lobster roll with Cape Cod Potato Chips.

WAREHAM'S CRANBERRY HARVEST CELEBRATION

Cranberries are an important crop in Massachusetts. They grow in wet soil called bogs. The bogs are flooded with water at harvest time. The cranberries float to the top. Then they are picked off their vines!

Wareham has a Cranberry Harvest Celebration in October. You can walk through the cranberries in waders. Those are pants that you can wear in the water!

Many Massachusetts farmers grow flowers and bushes. People buy them for their homes and yards. Dairy farmers raise cows for their milk. They sell the milk to many other states. Some milk is used to make milk chocolate. Want a really tasty treat? Dip some dried cranberries in milk chocolate!

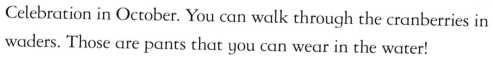

Massachusetts farmers harvest their cranberry crop. That's a lot of berries!

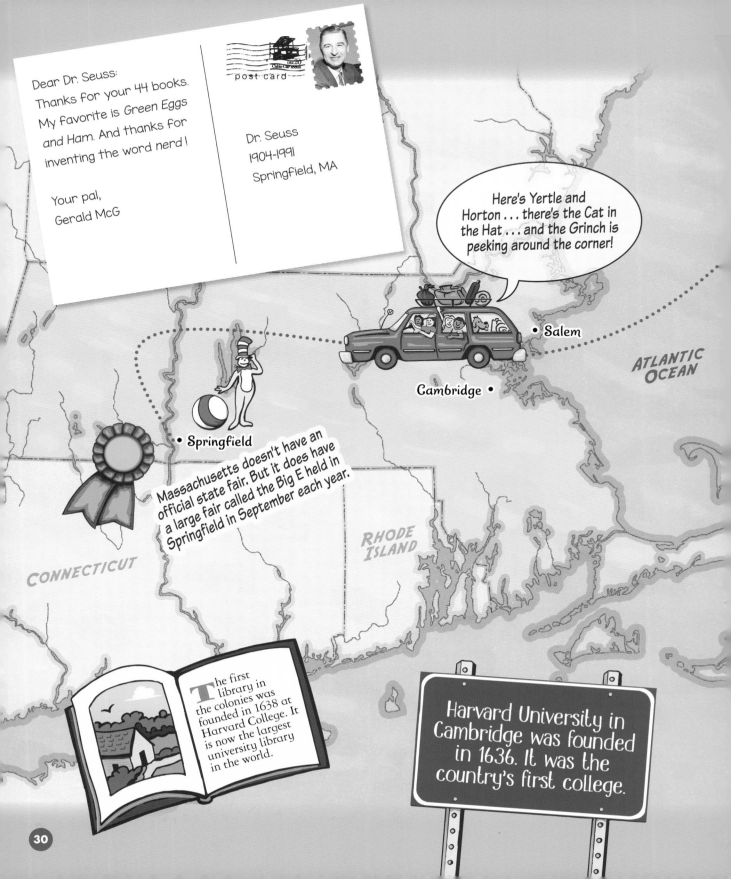

Dear Dr. Seuss:
Thanks for your 44 books. My favorite is Green Eggs and Ham. And thanks for inventing the word nerd!

Your pal,
Gerald McG

post card

Dr. Seuss
1904-1991
Springfield, MA

Here's Yertle and Horton . . . there's the Cat in the Hat . . . and the Grinch is peeking around the corner!

• Salem

ATLANTIC OCEAN

Cambridge •

• Springfield

Massachusetts doesn't have an official state fair. But it does have a large fair called the Big E held in Springfield in September each year.

RHODE ISLAND

CONNECTICUT

The first library in the colonies was founded in 1638 at Harvard College. It is now the largest university library in the world.

Harvard University in Cambridge was founded in 1636. It was the country's first college.

THE DR. SEUSS NATIONAL MEMORIAL SCULPTURE GARDEN

The Dr. Seuss National Memorial Sculpture Garden is in Springfield. It has more than a dozen life-size Dr. Seuss figures. Dr. Seuss was born in Springfield. His real name was Theodor Seuss Geisel. He used Springfield streets, parks, and people in his books!

Lots of other famous writers lived in Massachusetts. They include Louisa May Alcott and Edgar Allan Poe. Nathaniel Hawthorne was born in Salem. Many of his stories take place in Massachusetts.

Henry Wadsworth Longfellow and Emily Dickinson wrote poetry. Herman Melville sailed on ships from Massachusetts ports. He wrote *Moby Dick*. It's a story about a gigantic white whale.

This statue of the Lorax is just one of many at the Dr. Seuss National Memorial Sculpture Garden.

THE NAISMITH MEMORIAL BASKETBALL HALL OF FAME

Want to see Bob Lanier's basketball sneakers? They were a whopping size 22! Just visit the Basketball Hall of Fame in Springfield. You'll see lots of other basketball stuff there.

Bay Staters are wild about sports. Their own basketball team is the Boston Celtics. Massachusetts has four other **professional** teams. They play baseball, football, hockey, and soccer.

You can have plenty of fun in the Bay State. Just head for the coast. It's great for swimming, fishing, and boating.

In the winter, people ski down the snowy mountains. Are you a scaredy-cat on skis? Don't worry. There are lots of bunny hills for you!

The Naismith Memorial Basketball Hall of Fame opened in 1968.

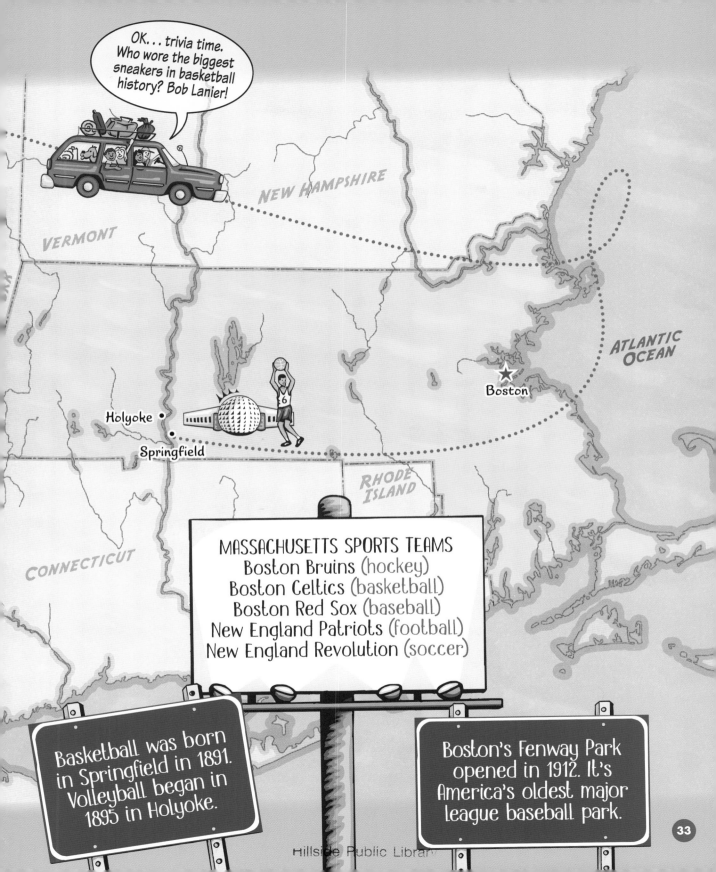

OK... trivia time. Who wore the biggest sneakers in basketball history? Bob Lanier!

NEW HAMPSHIRE

VERMONT

ATLANTIC OCEAN

Boston

Holyoke

Springfield

RHODE ISLAND

CONNECTICUT

MASSACHUSETTS SPORTS TEAMS
Boston Bruins (hockey)
Boston Celtics (basketball)
Boston Red Sox (baseball)
New England Patriots (football)
New England Revolution (soccer)

Basketball was born in Springfield in 1891. Volleyball began in 1895 in Holyoke.

Boston's Fenway Park opened in 1912. It's America's oldest major league baseball park.

GREENFIELD'S GRAVITY HILL

Suppose an apple falls off a tree. It rolls downhill, right? Not on Gravity Hill!

Gravity Hill is a strange place in Greenfield. If you were to drive there and put your car in neutral it will roll—uphill! So what's going on?

Some people say the land is really sloping downhill. It just *looks* like it's uphill. This has to do with the surrounding landscape. But others say ghosts are pushing the cars. Scientists are still trying to figure out this mystery. Meanwhile, got any ideas?

Most people say Gravity Hill is just an optical illusion.

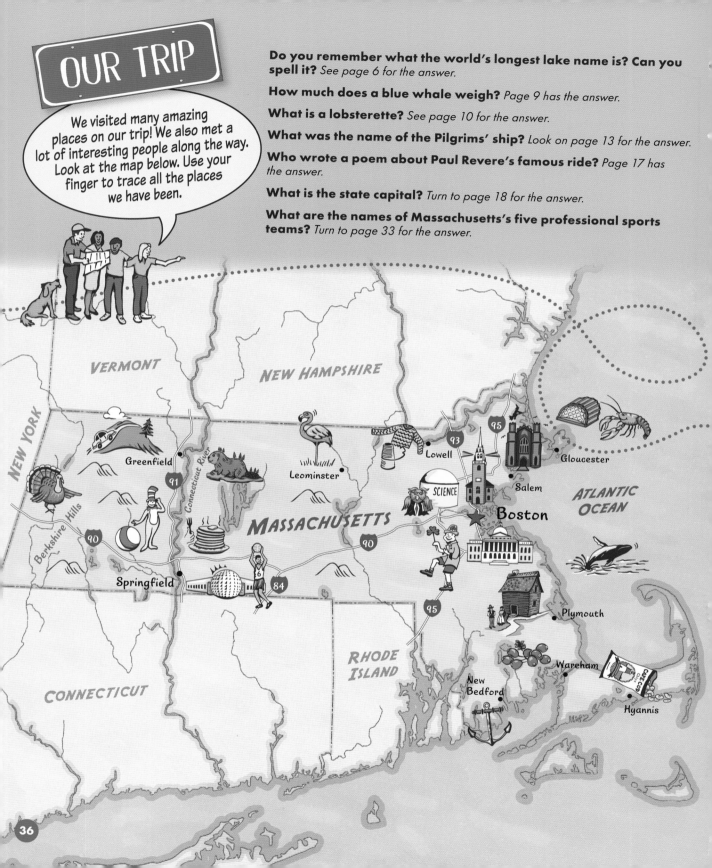

OUR TRIP

We visited many amazing places on our trip! We also met a lot of interesting people along the way. Look at the map below. Use your finger to trace all the places we have been.

Do you remember what the world's longest lake name is? Can you spell it? *See page 6 for the answer.*

How much does a blue whale weigh? *Page 9 has the answer.*

What is a lobsterette? *See page 10 for the answer.*

What was the name of the Pilgrims' ship? *Look on page 13 for the answer.*

Who wrote a poem about Paul Revere's famous ride? *Page 17 has the answer.*

What is the state capital? *Turn to page 18 for the answer.*

What are the names of Massachusetts's five professional sports teams? *Turn to page 33 for the answer.*

STATE SYMBOLS

State berry: Cranberry

State beverage: Cranberry juice

State bird: Black-capped chickadee

State building rock and monument stone: Granite

State cat: Tabby cat

State ceremonial march: "The Road to Boston"

State cookie: Chocolate chip cookie

State dessert: Boston cream pie

State dog: Boston terrier

State explorer rock: Dighton rock

State fish: Cod

State seal

STATE SONG

"ALL HAIL TO MASSACHUSETTS"
Words and music by Arthur J. Marsh

All hail to Massachusetts, the land of the free and the brave!
For Bunker Hill and Charlestown, and flag we love to wave;
For Lexington and Concord, and the shot heard 'round the world;
All hail to Massachusetts, we'll keep her flag unfurled.
She stands upright for freedom's light that shines from sea to sea;
All hail to Massachusetts! Our country 'tis of thee!

All hail to grand old Bay State, the home of the bean and the cod,
Where pilgrims found a landing and gave their thanks to God.
A land of opportunity in the good old U.S.A.

Where men live long and prosper, and people come to stay.
Don't sell her short but learn to court her industry and stride;
All hail to grand old Bay State! The land of pilgrim's pride!

All hail to Massachusetts, renowned in the Hall of Fame!
How proudly wave her banners emblazoned with her name!
In unity and brotherhood, sons and daughters go hand in hand;
All hail to Massachusetts, there is no finer land!
It's M-A-S-S-A-C-H-U-S-E-T-T-S.
All hail to Massachusetts! All hail! All hail! All hail!

That was a great trip! We have traveled all over Massachusetts! There are a few places that we didn't have time for, though. Next time, we plan to have breakfast in Springfield. That's where the World's Largest Pancake Breakfast is held every May. More than 60,000 pancakes are served at this event.

State flag

FAMOUS PEOPLE

Adams, John (1735–1826), 2nd U.S. president

Adams, John Quincy (1767–1848), 6th U.S. president

Adams, Samuel (1722–1803), politician during the American Revolution

Alcott, Louisa May (1832–1888), author

Anthony, Susan B. (1820–1906), reformer

Attucks, Crispus (ca.1723–1770), patriot during the American Revolution

Bernstein, Leonard (1918–1990), composer and conductor

Bradford, William (1590–1657), Pilgrim leader

Bush, George H. W. (1924–), 41st U.S. president

Cena, John (1997–), wrestler and actor

Dickinson, Emily (1830–1886), poet

Geisel, Theodor Seuss (1904–1991), children's author

Hancock, John (1737–1793), first person to sign the Declaration of Independence

Kennedy, John F. (1917–1963), 35th U.S. president

Lyon, Mary (1797–1849), educator and founder of the first U.S. woman's college

Poe, Edgar Allan (1809–1849), author

Poehler, Amy (1971–), actress

Raisman, Aly (1994–), Olympic gymnast

Revere, Paul (1735–1818), silversmith and patriot during the American Revolution

Samoset (ca. 1590–ca. 1653), Abenaki chief and friend of the Pilgrims

Squanto (1585–ca. 1622) Member of the Patuxet tribe and interpreter for the Pilgrims

Trainor, Meghan (1993–), singer and songwriter

Wahlberg, Mark (1971–), actor and rapper

WORDS TO KNOW

ancestors (AN-cess-turz) family members who lived long ago

colonists (KOL-uh-nists) people who settle a new land for their country

colony (KOL-uh-nee) land that has been settled by people from another country and that is ruled by that country

commonwealth (KOM-uhn-welth) a government for the good of all its people

immigrants (IM-uh-gruhnts) people who move from their home country to another country

industries (IN-duh-streez) types of business

lookout (LOOK-out) a person who watches for something

professional (pruh-FESH-uh-nuhl) doing an activity for pay

settlement (SET-uhl-muhnt) a new land with ties to a parent country

steeple (STEE-puhl) a tall, pointy tower on a church

textile (TEK-stile) cloth

TO LEARN MORE

IN THE LIBRARY

Bauer, Marion Dane. *Celebrating Massachusetts*. Boston, MA: Houghton Mifflin Harcourt, 2014.

Cunningham, Kevin. *The Massachusetts Colony*. New York, NY: Scholastic, 2011.

Edwards, Roberta. *Who Was Paul Revere?* New York, NY: Grosset & Dunlap, 2011.

ON THE WEB
Visit our Web site for links about Massachusetts:
childsworld.com/links

Note to Parents, Teachers, and Librarians: We routinely verify our Web links to make sure they are safe and active sites. So encourage your readers to check them out!

PLACES TO VISIT OR CONTACT
Massachusetts Historical Society
masshist.org
1154 Boylston Street
Boston, MA 02215
617/536-1608
For more information about the history of Massachusetts

Massachusetts Office of Travel & Tourism
massvacation.com
10 Park Plaza, Suite 4510
Boston, MA 02116
617/973-8500
For more information about traveling in Massachusetts

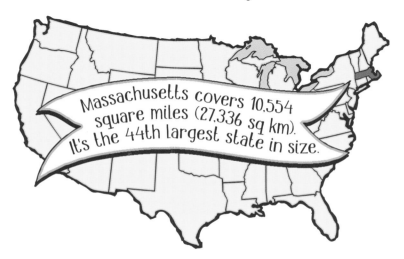

Massachusetts covers 10,554 square miles (27,336 sq km). It's the 44th largest state in size.

INDEX

Bye, Bay State. We had a great time. We'll come back soon!